Selling in a Recession:

21 Tips and Strategies for Finding New
Business in a Tough Economy

by Matthew Aaron

"If you're in sales, then stop worrying about the economy and pick up a copy of this book now!"

Debbie Allen, author of Confessions of Shameless Self Promoters

"If you're in sales you need to read Selling in a Recession: 21 Tips and Strategies to Grow Your Business in a Tough Economy by Matthew Aaron. This insightful and easy to read book will not only help you to think about the current economy with new eyes, it will also help your sales."

Shawna Schuh, Certified Speaking Professional and Profitable People Skills Expert

"This book is a must read immediately. Things are a challenge in this economy for any of us with the responsibility to sell. Matt helps us not only understand the situation, but also tells us what to do about it now."

Thomas J. Winninger, Best-Selling Author of Price Wars

"The way to identify a 'recession' is to look for a lack of sales. Matthew Aaron shows you how to do exactly the opposite. He shows you how to find the opportunities and make the sales despite the economy. This thoughtfully written book is spot-on with its recommendations and tips. I suggest that you make it your constant companion while growing your sales as others are cowering in fear."

Jim Cathcart, Motivational Speaker and Author of Relationship Selling.

Cover Design by Steve Dickenson
Book Design/Back Cover by Nichole Ward, Morrison Alley Design

First Printing 2009
ISBN 978-0-9817088-1-2
Library of Congress Control Number: 2009922141

For my parents, Bob and Mary, who taught me the number one lesson in sales and life:

Never give up, because you never know when something great is just around the corner

Contents

INTRODUCTION

At the time of this writing, the economy is once again the focal point of most people's attention. As one sector after another rolls through job cuts, bankruptcies, and government bailout packages, many are starting to wonder *how will I make it through?*

This is especially true for salespeople, who count on commissions and new business for their livelihood. Unlike doctors or accountants, who might feel the pinch but generally keep collecting their salaries, the men and women in sales have no margin for error. They don't have the luxury of waiting for things to pick up – they need to make something happen now.

This also holds true for others who don't consider themselves professional salespeople, but still need to draw in new customers and orders to stay afloat. So, while the majority of this book is addressed to people in sales, the same advice applies to business owners, sales managers, executives, and the self-employed. That's because despite your respective job titles, you're all wrestling with the same issue: how to bring in more business when there's less business to be had.

Rest assured, you'll find answers in these pages. Best of all, they aren't going to be complicated or academic; they're real-world strategies that can work for anyone willing to apply them. I won't try to sugarcoat the truth – recessions *are* difficult and sometimes painful – but I'm also going to show you the other side of the coin. Like the Chinese symbol that embodies both danger and opportunity, recessions bring trouble and instability while at the same time offering savvy professionals the chance to increase their customer base and position themselves for the future.

So, let go of your fear and anxiety for a moment and let's get started. Remember, a recession is like rain. It might spoil your day at the park, but it's necessary in order for living things to grow. Keeping that perspective can help you tackle a soft economy head-on while the people around you focus on the negative.

With that in mind, let's take a look at what a recession is, and how you can sell through one...

CHAPTER ONE
SELLING IN A RECESSION

Selling is hard enough in any economy because there's no safety net. You get paid for what you bring in, not how many hours you show up.

When a flood comes, it's the people who live on the first floor who worry first. I think that's as apt an analogy as any to describe what it's like to sell during a recession. That's because the men and women who make their living from commissions – the professionals who stand at the forefront of nearly all economic activity – are the first to feel the effects of a slowdown.

What's more, they do it without any kind of safety net. They're paid for the business they bring in, so there's no cushy salary to count on when things are going wrong. Their only option is to keep plugging forward and find a way to bring in new accounts. It might not be easy, but the alternatives are either to work for peanuts, or to give up and try to find another job.

The matter is made that much harder by the fact that many professional salespeople have never been through a recession before. For one thing, companies tend to hire when the economy is on an upswing. For the most part, new producers are trained and acclimated in an easy sales climate. And at the same time, those salespeople who aren't firmly established in their careers tend to leave for safer pastures when a slow economy hits. In this way, recession often has the effect of clearing out the weaker salespeople in the company or industry. This might sound scary, and it can be, but it also means that there are more opportunities for those who stick with it.

So the first rule of a recession is *don't panic*. If you're newer to the field, take comfort in the knowledge that you can make it through. In fact, by using the tools in this book, you might gain a leg up on some of the more experienced veterans around your office. On the other hand, if you've seen a recession or two in your sales career, I invite you to read through these chapters as well. I meet lots of salespeople who don't understand what a recession is, or how to get through one. It's likely that you've come to think of them as painful contractions, when the reality is that they're a good chance to expand your customer base.

Recessions are nothing new. Business cycles have been with us for hundreds of years or longer, and they're not likely to go away anytime soon. Sure, politicians promise to end them and economists look for ways around them, but the simple fact is that our economy is a behemoth – and a living one at that. It labors day in and day out, producing goods and services all over the world. With all that activity, it's no wonder it catches the sniffles once in a while.

In the next chapter, we'll look at what a recession is and isn't, but let me take a moment to clear up a misconception: not everything about a recession is bad. I know what you're thinking – less money and fewer jobs sure sounds bad. And in that sense you're right; a declining economy does mean things are a bit tougher and tighter. But at the same time, it's also a chance to get slimmer, stronger, and more efficient for the future. It's also a good window to find accounts and business that would be hard to bring in otherwise.

That's the second important point about a recession, and one that we'll come back to again and again in this book – a recession is a great time to reposition yourself and your business by becoming leaner, more efficient, and more competitive. As a result, you can not only pick up new clients and business in the short term, but set yourself up for long-term success. In other words, you might have to tighten your belt for a while, but you'll come out stronger for the wear and tear.

Much of your success or failure in a recession is going to stem from how you view your economic climate. If you see it as an inevitable source of pain and loss, then that's probably what you're going to get. On the other hand, if you recognize it as a chance to try some new things and outmaneuver your competitors, then you're probably going to make it through in good shape.

Now, let's get started by taking a look at what a recession actually is. Often, the easiest way to increase our confidence is by understanding what's behind our fear. Besides, you might just find that a recession isn't quite as scary as you thought...

CHAPTER TWO

UNDERSTAND THE SITUATION

Most salespeople don't understand what a recession really means, and so they make decisions that make things worse, not better.

Ask most people what they think about the economy, and they're likely to meet you with a blank stare or a few comments about the stock market. But mention the mere possibility of a recession, and you'll bring out every brand of gloom and doom: lost jobs, lower pay, and an assortment of other financial plagues. The reality, though, is that most people fail to understand what a recession is and isn't. For that reason, they tend to overreact or make decisions that actually work against them during a downturn.

All of this begs the question – *what is a recession, actually?* Well, let's start with the "official" definition and work backwards. In most economics textbooks, a recession is defined by two or more quarters of declining economic activity. That really clears things up, doesn't it?

Let's dissect these terms and see what we're really talking about. First off, a quarter is nothing more than a three-month period; so two quarters would be half a year. Economic activity is a bit harder to define. There are a lot of complicated formulas and equations that economists use to try to figure out what's going on in the world, but what they really amount to is the total amount of buying and selling going on.

To understand this in the most basic sense, imagine that you like to buy yourself a giant cup of coffee every morning. Out of the few dollars you spend, some of that money goes to the owner of the coffee shop. Other small amounts make their way to the coffee farmers, dairy and sugar producers, and the employees of the coffee shop, not to mention the utility companies, commodities brokers, banks, insurance companies, paper cup manufacturers, and dozens of other entities that support the business directly or indirectly. So each time you buy that cup of coffee, you're creating economic activity for all of those groups, not to mention all of the people that they buy from, and so on, and so on.

Now, if you imagine the same thing for all the purchases and investments you decide to make for a few months, along with all the purchases and investments that *millions of other people* have also made in that time, you have a picture of the economy as a whole. If you had an easy time following the first example, and a hard time wrapping your mind around everything in the second, then you can see why it's so difficult for people to understand what's going on across the economy, much less make solid predictions.

That's where all of those complicated equations come in. By studying things like the price of a gallon of milk, the number of new cars sold, or how many people filed for unemployment in a given month, economists can draw some assumptions about the bigger picture. In other words, they can come up with numbers to make sense of all of those billions of purchases. These are the statistics you see and read most often in the financial news – the GDP's, consumer price indexes, and consumer confidence levels of the world. In each case, they're just a collection of data designed to tell you how much buying and selling is going on out there, and at what prices.

The key point to get out of all of this is that when you see figures and percentages in the news, they represent an average. That is, they are a snapshot of what's been going on over the last few weeks or months when things are examined from a distance. When most of those numbers are getting bigger, we call it a "growth" or a "good economy." But when things are moving backwards, the "r" word rears its ugly head. All that basically means, though, is that as a whole we are buying and selling less than we were before.

Notice that I didn't say *how much* less than before. Some recessions are quite mild, representing more of a pause in growth than an actual decline. You've probably been through one or two of these in the past: not many people are losing their jobs, but they aren't exactly rushing out to invest in luxury autos, either. In the case of a more severe recession, however, the effects run a bit deeper. There's real fear about the future in nearly every part of the economy; job losses are more widespread, and the effects are felt all around the country as even the biggest companies lose ground or close altogether.

In both cases, though, there's still quite a bit of economic activity to be found. A light recession, for example, might bring a 2% decline in economic activity. That's a noticeable change, but it also means 98% of the economy is still intact. So, even though the country is going into recession, we're still firing on almost all cylinders. In fact, this still holds true even in a more severe recession. Most people would consider a 5 -10% drop in economic production to be a pretty nasty time indeed. And yet, even in this dire circumstance, at least nine tenths of all that buying and selling is still in place.

Also remember that we said these numbers are taken from the economy as a whole. Just because one company or area is affected doesn't mean that all others will be – even in the same industry or geographic area. For one thing, certain types of businesses are always more likely to feel the pinch in a recession than others. For instance, those businesses that get by on selling luxuries or premium purchases that people can do without in tough times are likely to see the biggest and most immediate hit. Again, common sense is at play here. Few people rush out to buy a home theater system when they're not expecting their regular commision check or annual bonus, let alone when they're worried about losing their job.

In fact, for those same reasons, there are certain types of companies that actually do *better* during a recession. How could this be? Well, one of the most obvious reasons is that during tough times, people often look to substitute one product or activity for another in order to save money. As an example, think of things you'd buy in a grocery store. In a soft economy, families looking for a place to save a few extra dollars might skip going out for dinner once in awhile. But they aren't going to stop eating altogether, no matter what's going in with the world, so they're likely to spend that money at their local market instead.

Likewise, some organizations are just going to do a better job than others of finding new customers and offering their services during a downturn. These shifts are less predictable, because they aren't driven by pure economics, but they still happen. Just as some salespeople will come out winners in a recession while some will struggle, companies are going to compete amongst themselves for the remaining business. Some are going to lose, and maybe even go out of business. But the winners are going to do very well, because they're operating with less competition than before.

In the next chapter, we are going to look at ways you can find those customers that are doing well in a soft economy. For now though, just recognize that a recession means that belts are being tightened – not that all buying and selling is going to cease. There's still plenty of business out there to be found, as long as you're willing to look for it.

CHAPTER THREE
FIND THE MONEY

There are businesses and industries that actually make more money during a recession. Finding them is a good way to increase your sales.

In the last chapter, we talked about the economy as a way of thinking about the billions of small transactions that take place every day. The point to walk away with was that even in a soft economy there are going to be people and companies that are doing well – sometimes very well.

If you're still a little skeptical of that idea, think of it this way: when a hurricane comes to town, that's pretty bad for everybody, right? After all, big storms can do millions or even billions of dollars worth of damage and destruction, putting a strain on homeowners, city governments, and insurance companies alike. If you think about it, though, hurricanes mean more than one kind of windfall for a few specific groups. Hardware stores, for one, do record business at the first sign of trouble by selling boards, bags of sand, and other items people buy to prepare for emergencies. Handymen, landscapers, and cleanup crews are likewise poised to pick up new customers as homeowners look to rebuild spaces that have been damaged. So do grocery stores, once again, who sell the fresh water and canned goods that suddenly come into style with a big storm warning. So you see, even in the face of an event that most would consider to be an economic catastrophe, there are people and businesses who stand to benefit.

A recession is the same way. Although each economic storm is different – recessions vary in the specific sectors of the economy that are hit, how long they last, and how far they spread – there are going to be some companies that are well-positioned to come out ahead. Some, like collection agencies or job-placement services, are obvious candidates to see a spike in business as incomes decrease; they're simply set up to help businesses or job seekers in trouble. Others will succeed because their management and sales arms find new ways of reaching out to people, or change the way they do business.

Traditionally, fields like medicine, education, and energy are all relatively safe industries during a downturn. To that list, you could also add utility companies, grocery stores and discount retailers. Again, there's no complicated reasoning here: even when money is tight, people continue to spend on things like food, gas and prescription drugs. And workers who have been laid off are likely to look at more schooling as a way of finding a new job. So, if you're looking for new customers in a tight economy, these are all good places to start.

And just as recessions don't hit industries evenly, neither do they land in every part of the country with the same force. Certain areas, by virtue of the types of businesses that they foster and support, are barely going to feel the bump. Others, seeing their largest employers and suppliers cut back or go under, are going to be much more effected than the nation as a whole. And, of course, the same holds true across borders and even continents. In a general sense, what's bad for one economy is bad for another. But that's not always the case, especially when you consider competing currencies and products. A recession in the U.S., for example, typically weakens the dollar and makes American products cheaper overseas. Knowing how one specific area or country is doing compared to others can be a good way of finding new places to sell.

Keep in mind these are only general guidelines. The trick to finding money in a recession isn't in finding a list of companies that are doing well; the real key is thinking things through a few steps. That's because every purchase, even those that *aren't* made, benefits someone else. For example, one of the first victims of a recession is likely to be a car dealership. Not many people think about upgrading their personal automobiles when they're worried about keeping their jobs or saving more for the future. Most salespeople would recognize this fact, get discouraged about dealing with any businesses that have to do with cars, and stop their thinking there. But by going the next step, you might wonder about where those dollars are going, if they aren't making it to the dealership. Instead of investing in new automobiles, many families will opt to keep and maintain their current automobiles. So who does this benefit? Mechanics and service stations, for one.

This is only one example, but you could probably think of dozens just like it. That's because almost everybody's been in the position of having to tighten their budget before. So take that thinking and apply it to your customers. Where will they look to save money? Which purchases will they put off? What are they likely to buy or use instead? Once you know the answers to these questions, you're well on your way to riding out the recession.

And on the other side of the coin, actively seek out those clients who were doing as well or better than before. Start by checking out the local business news and press releases. We'll talk about this kind of research in a later chapter, and how you can use it to figure out which businesses are flying high. But don't stop there; look beyond the obvious. The money and customers are still out there, and in fact, you're probably in a better position to find them, even though they're well-hidden. Why? Because when things are going well, it's easy for any salesperson to pick up the paper and decide who to call. But when things are tight, only the more innovative professionals are going to find new sales and new business. That means you have to work harder to find each and every account, but when you do, there's going to be far less competition.

Remember, a recession is nothing more than an economic storm. To the smart salesperson, this just means it's time to start calling on the umbrella factory.

CHAPTER FOUR
MAKE MORE ROOM

One of the easiest ways to make selling easier in a bad economy is by reducing the pressure to make a sale.

Conventional wisdom states that in a recession, the best thing to do is decrease your expenses. This is sound financial advice for anyone, but for salespeople, it's worth its weight in gold. Why? Because the mental edge is a major component of a strong sales career, especially when times are tough.

Selling is not an easy job under any circumstances. But when you really need to make something happen, it's almost impossible. Put another way, it's incredibly difficult to sell anything at any price when you really need to make a sale. It's almost as if people can hear and feel your desperation. If you've ever been in a situation where you desperately needed a commission to make your mortgage or pay a bill, then you know what I'm talking about. The added pressure of knowing you have to move something makes things that much harder.

On the other hand, making a sale isn't nearly as tough when you don't need one. As ironic and unfair as that may seem, it's just a psychological reality. Success breeds more success; people want to work with and buy from other people who seem confident in what they're doing. That's why one big sale, or a bunch of little ones, can put you on a roll. With your quotas met and your bank account secure, it's easy to call on new customers and open new accounts. The pressure's off, and so the work comes easily.

For that reason, one of the best things salespeople can do for themselves at the start of a recession is to decrease their personal expenses. This works for big items in your budget, as well as small ones. Canceling the wine of the month membership or cutting back on the amount of lattes you drink is a good start, but putting off that new luxury car purchase is probably a good idea, too.

The point isn't that you're necessarily going to have less money – in fact, many salespeople who follow the advice in this book can actually do better in a recession than they would have otherwise – but that you relieve the mental pressure that comes with having a huge stack of bills in a declining economy. Coming into the office stressed about your finances leaves you in a position where it's going to be very difficult to find the new customers you need. Conversely, knowing that you are going to be fine one way or the other puts you in the free and relaxed state of mind that leads to breakout selling.

So look for places in your monthly budget where you can cut out the unnecessary. Give extra thought to your magazine subscriptions, expensive car payments, and entertainment services you don't need. At the same time, go through your bank statements and see how well you've been taking care of your money. Do you have some savings? Are you feeding an expensive shopping habit? Finding places to cut fat from your budget is never easy or enjoyable. After all, you're looking at taking away luxuries to which you have become accustomed. But if you're willing to put your long-term success ahead of your short-term comfort, then you'll probably find numerous places where you can cut back. Besides, most of the time you won't even miss the things you're doing without a few weeks later. It's like pulling off a Band-Aid; it only hurts for a second.

After you've gone through your personal finances, do the same thing at work. Look for places in your budget where you can cut expenses. Are you paying for leads that haven't panned out? An expensive advertising service, or set of high-end gifts for low margin customers? Are you spending a lot on golf memberships or other social and sporting events in the hopes of finding customers? Now is the time to scrutinize all of these expenses and decide which ones are profitable and which ones aren't.

Notice that you should do this even for items that aren't coming out of your own pocket. You might not think it's a big deal to charge a few frills on the company dime, but being thrifty with your employer's money during a downturn can help you as much as them. On the one hand, it shows your manager that you're paying attention, and that you're concerned about the company's well-being. If he or she is forced to lay off part of the sales force, who do you think is the more likely to be let go, the salesperson who cuts costs, or the one who charges expensive lunches like there's no tomorrow? By the same token, showing some smart fiscal sense is a good way to get noticed by top executives, who might just remember you when it's time for the next promotion or bonus.

Deciding to get by with less isn't easy, but it can actually help you to come out of a recession with a lot more money than you had going in. Make things easier on yourself and relieve some mental pressure by cutting back. It might not feel good at first, but you'll sell more and sleep easier.

CHAPTER FIVE
THINK SMALL

Even in a recession, your customers are going to continue to make hundreds of small purchases that can keep your business growing.

In the earlier chapters, we made much of the fact that a recession means an economic slowdown, not a complete stop. In other words, most of the decreased spending comes in the nonessentials – the luxury cars, flat screen televisions, and five-star vacations – not in the everyday purchases and investments that go on regardless of what the economy is doing.

This applies whether you sell to households or businesses. Most companies, as well as families, will look to put off major investments during a recession. At the same time, they'll continue making the hundreds of small purchases that keep their day to day lives and operations going. By recognizing this and changing their focus, the astute salesperson can put aside their proposals with the longest odds and focus on the small deals that are right in front of them.

In a practical sense, this usually means looking for a number of smaller sales instead of one really big one. A software dealer, for example, might look to sell upgrades instead of completely new packages. Or a medical equipment account executive might send proposals for remanufactured machines, instead of brand-new models fresh off the line.

In both cases, the point is to replace your larger sales with smaller ones. That's because, generally speaking, you're going to have a hard time convincing people to undergo a major purchase. For one thing, they've probably got less cash to go around. It's also likely they're concerned about the impact that any short or long-term financing will have on their future cash flow. But most of all, they're probably just afraid. Recessions amount to a shortage of confidence as much as they do a shortage of actual cash. That means that any large proposal is likely to meet with a number of objections, and you'll never be able to overcome the biggest one, which is insecurity about future income.

Looking for smaller sales sounds easy enough, but what if you deal in those luxury goods that people are going to put off buying? Is there any way out of the recession trap? Actually, there is. The trick isn't in trying to continue to make the big sales – that's likely to be an uphill battle – but in moving product accessories to existing customers. Plenty of cars, yachts, and other big-ticket items are sold in a normal economy. And most of those folks don't stop owning their favorite toys just because incomes have dipped. So, while they might put off buying the next big thing, they're still going to need tires, maintenance and warranties for the things they already own.

If you're thinking that it's going to be a lot harder making a good living selling tires than German cars, you're right. To get by on a strategy like this requires that you increase your activity a great deal. And as a matter of fact, we're going to take a look at ways to do that in just a moment. But looking on the bright side, while shooting for smaller sales might mean more calls and proposals, it also generally means less haggling and a much higher closing percentage. People who stress out about spending tens or hundreds of thousands of dollars, whether it's their company's money or their own, feel a lot more comfortable writing small checks. So, even though you might have to find more new customers, you'll probably devote a lot less time to each one. And, as an added bonus, you'll come out of the recession with a much larger customer base. So when the economy – and all those large purchases – come back in full force, who do you think they'll turn to when they're ready to buy?

Smart salespeople adjust to a sour economy by giving their customers what they want, and what they can afford. It's a lot easier to find five small clients in a recession than it is to get one big one. So go looking where the money is – in the small sales – and you won't just survive a recession, you'll come out the other side with a longer client list.

CHAPTER SIX
GET BUSY

There's always more business to be found, if you're willing to look hard enough.

One of the easiest ways to get through a recession is by doing more. Sounds simple, doesn't it? But, the fact of the matter is it works. Here's why: as we saw in Chapter Two, a recession is nothing more than a net decrease in economic activity. In other words, it means people are buying just a bit less. By knowing how much less, we can work backwards and figure out what we need to do to overcome it.

Economists like to measure the severity of a downturn by how many jobs are lost, how many new homes are being built, and watching the prices of certain items. Taken individually, they often under or overstate what's going on in the economy, or miss the point altogether. Collectively, though, they do a pretty good job of telling us what's going on.

So, when we see it reported that the economy has slipped by one or two percent, we get a convenient snapshot of what's actually happening in the world – people are buying one or two percent less than they were before. So if you multiply your efforts by that much, you're likely to continue earning and selling exactly as much as you are now.

To illustrate this point, let's put our example into some hard numbers. Let's say that you're used to selling twenty units of whatever you sell every month; whether it's cars, high-yield bonds, or toasters isn't important. What matters is that you're selling twenty of them. Now, let's assume that we're in the midst of a recession that sees most industries lose about five percent of their business – by all accounts, a pretty nasty environment.

Depending on what you sell, this could show itself in a few ways. On the one hand, you might see your customers placing smaller orders with you. Or, maybe you work with a product that isn't easily divided, but you're getting fewer overall sales. Either way, it's very likely that you're facing a five percent cut in pay, so if you're going to keep making as much money as you have been, you're going to have to find a way to replace those missing orders. Luckily, it shouldn't be too hard to figure out where to find them.

Losing five percent of your business, whether through smaller orders or fewer buyers, means that you have to find one more customer per month to make up the difference (Remember, we assumed you were starting out with twenty). Suppose you know that it takes you, on average, three appointments to generate one new customer. You also know that it takes you twenty cold calls to set those three appointments. To keep your sales from dropping off, then, you simply need to make twenty more calls per month, or about one per working day. Doing so over time will virtually guarantee that you won't feel the pinch of a bad economy. Imagine what would happen with two calls, or five?

Two important points need to be made here. The first is that these percentages can be fluid, but the results never are. It may turn out that during a recession, you need to make twenty-five calls to get three appointments, or that you find you need four appointments to close a sale. But the basic premise remains the same: keep doing what you need to do, and you'll always hit your numbers. Most salespeople don't fail in a bad business climate because there aren't buyers to be found; they fail because they become too discouraged to look for them.

The second point is that for any of this to work, you have to know what your numbers look like. In other words, you need to be keeping track of your activity. Doing so allows you to get a clear picture of what's going on at any given moment. Have you been making enough contacts? Do you have a realistic shot at reaching your monthly sales goal? No matter how busy you feel, the figures will never lie. By keeping good records, you can easily see which of your efforts are working and where the bulk of your results are coming from consistently.

Another reason keeping track of activity is so important, though, is a little more subtle: *the more you keep track of what you do, the more motivated you become to do the right thing.* Anybody who's ever been on a diet that required them to keep a food log can tell you exactly what I mean. It's one thing to have a piece of chocolate cake and then try to forget about it. It's another thing to pick up that fork knowing that you'll have to write down that you did so later. This works, by the way, even if nobody else is going to see what you've written down. The act of keeping a record creates accountability; it forces us to come face-to-face with how we are spending our time and what decisions we're making.

For salespeople, this is absolutely critical. Nobody, when the end of the week comes, wants to see that they've done nothing with their time. Instead of wasting an hour reading the paper, making a few calls seems like a better idea. This is especially true if they're going to have to report those results to the team or a manager, or post them on a common board.

Have you been keeping track of your activity closely for the last few years? If you haven't, you're certainly not alone. When things are good, there is a tendency for salespeople to become lazy. That's only natural; there's a lot of money floating around, so nobody has to work quite as hard to earn their commission checks. Pretty soon bad habits set in, and the first thing to suffer is activity. They make less outbound calls and make fewer contacts, and generally aren't as diligent about finding business as they could be. But since they're hitting all their monthly and quarterly sales goals, there doesn't seem to be any reason to obsess about whether they've made five cold calls this week, or asked for three referrals.

But once a recession sets in these bad habits stick around. The sales team is no longer used to doing the hard work of bringing in new business, because there's been little or no activity going on beyond catering to existing customers and fielding leads that come into the office. And so they're hit twice as hard as they would have been otherwise. On the one hand, the economy has gone sour and they aren't getting the kind of business they're used to. On the other hand, their pipelines are empty because they haven't been actively working on new prospects or undertaking any outgoing marketing efforts.

Obviously the answer to both of these problems is to increase activity. They have to do the hard work of setting goals – whether it be a certain number of calls, e-mails, or in-person consultations each day – and then do whatever it takes to meet them. Remember, *numbers don't lie*. Keep doing enough to get the business, and you'll always have business, no matter what the economy is doing.

If you're skeptical about this advice, give it a try. Work out how many calls, contacts or appointments you think you need to make to bring in five new clients, and then go and do it. I guarantee you'll find what the most successful salespeople already know – that sales activity always leads to a predictable result. By putting more in, you'll always get more out, regardless of the economy.

CHAPTER SEVEN
ADAPT YOUR OFFER

One of the keys to getting through a recession is understanding your customer's mindset.

By now, you're probably starting to realize that a recession is about a lot more than a small percentage decline in overall economic activity. For most people, it's not about inflation, lost jobs, or companies closing their doors. Certainly, these things effect people's mindsets – especially the owners and employees in question. But still, what's at the heart of the problem isn't dollars and cents; it's *fear*.

The fear of loss is a lot stronger than the desire to gain, and this fact is never more apparent than it is during tough economic times. By tailoring their approach to this mindset – helping people keep what they have, instead of trying to convince them to reach for more – top salespeople can find a new way to engage their clients and prospects, not to mention provide an invaluable service.

Getting started is easy. Look for areas in your business where you can help people to protect what they already have. A financial consultant might pitch safer investments and government-backed bonds; an insurance producer might offer fixed annuities or health care coverage; a utilities company could sell prepaid heating plans. Any of these are likely to be profitable because a recession shifts people's thinking away from what they have, and towards what they're afraid to *lose*.

Don't underestimate the power of such an adjustment. For all of our sophistications, humans still have a tendency to act with a herd mentality. It's normal to be scared about economic troubles that are largely out of our control. This is only enhanced by modern economic media coverage, which spreads bad news like wildfire into homes night after night. Before long, concern turns to worry, which can quickly lead to a sense of pervasive doom. In other words, a small recession leads to fears of a much bigger one, and people act and buy accordingly. Instead of looking for the next greatest thing, they try to hold on to what they've worked so hard for already. In other words, they stop shopping for a ladder and start looking for a safety net.

But before you rush out to start selling products and services that cater to people's fear, you might be asking yourself: *is this manipulative?* Is it wrong to profit from the uncertainty in a recession? I think the answer to that question depends a great deal on what you are actually selling, and your motives behind it. If you're out to fleece people for a quick buck, then you already know the answer and I'm not going to tell you anything to make you feel better about yourself. If, on the other hand, you sell a legitimate product that can help people protect themselves, their families, or the fruits of their hard work, then why should you feel bad about it? The heart of any good sales approach is giving people what they want. In a good economy, that might mean luxuries and big-ticket items. But during a recession, it can certainly mean a way to hold on to the things that they already have.

Take, for instance, the case of those government-backed bonds I mentioned a moment ago. While not the flashiest investment, they've been providing steady, reliable income to individuals and institutions alike for centuries. Providing these to concerned investors is no more unethical than selling celery stalks at a diet camp. You're simply finding people who are looking for a safe, healthy solution that meets their current needs. And if they didn't get it from you, they'll find another salesperson who is willing to amend their approach to the current climate.

Of course, there are always going to be those people who seek to profit from the misfortune of others. And they are usually easy to spot because their entire offer is based on little more than fear or outlandish promises. But I don't count them amongst the ranks of professional salespeople who take up the tough task of introducing new products and ideas to families and businesses in need. And within those professionals, there's the opportunity – and responsibility – to provide clients and customers with the right tools at the right time. So, if you're making a genuine effort to help the people you serve get what they need, then I don't think you need to be overly worried about doing something dishonest. Just tell the truth and let your conscience be your guide.

As you look for ways to grow your business during a recession, remember that psychology is an even greater force than simple math. The people you do business with probably aren't that interested in finding out what they can afford; they want to know how to afford the things they've already got. Help them find the answers to these questions, and offer solutions that keep them afloat in rough economic waters, and you'll throw a lifeline to yourself at the same time.

CHAPTER EIGHT
BRING OUT THE BARGAIN HUNTERS

Recessions bring out bargain buyers. Why not use that to your advantage?

If you've ever known someone who pinched every penny, saving for "a rainy day," then you've met the perfect recession prospect. That's because there are some people who live for a deal. These are the folks who don't want to buy anything unless it's from a fire sale. The bad news is that they didn't listen to anything you had to say when you first tried to sell to them. The good news is they've been waiting until now to buy, and they're flush with cash.

In Chapter Five, I advised you to abandon the search for big sales and focus on the small fish, and that's good advice... mostly. Finding customers who are profiting from the recession are one exception that we talked about earlier; bargain hunters are the other.

Chances are, these folks drove you nuts at some point in the past. That's because, no matter how hard you tried, you weren't able to price your product low enough to get them to part with their hard-earned money. Whatever your deal was, they wanted a better one. They might have been a big headache before, but now that the recession's come around, they can become your best friends.

These are the folks who want the best price – and I mean, the absolute, rock bottom best price – on everything. They've been waiting and waiting, watching prices fall in advertisements and on the Internet, and now they're probably ready to buy. Why? Not because anything's changed with your product or their needs, but because they can now make a purchase that will allow them to brag to their friends and family about how much less "than sticker" they paid.

In addition to being discount hounds, these folks tend to be fantastic savers. That's why they're so valuable now. At a time when most consumers are hurting, these men and women are flush with cash, and they're ready to use some of it. They know the world is on sale, and they want to take advantage of the deals that are going to come along. More often than not, they're even – or especially – looking to buy those products that won't seem to move at any price during a recession: cars, electronics, furniture, and other personal products. That's not to say that they don't exist in the business-to-business world, though, because they certainly do. There are millions of owners and managers out there, in companies of every size, who relish the thought of holding off their investments until prices have fallen to the floor.

Now is the time to reach out to all of them. If you've been keeping good records of your clients and prospects, you'll likely see a few immediate candidates – buyers who never stop beating you up over price, protecting every penny like it's a matter of personal pride.

Before you pull out the Rolodex, though, take a moment to formulate a sales strategy. Selling to these folks isn't quite as easy as saying that the economy is terrible, so they should come in and buy something. Remember, they're savoring the deal as much as they are the product. To that end, you should be ready with a number of reasons about why now is the ideal time to make a new purchase: you're running out of space to store your stock, a product line is going to be discontinued, you're having a once-in-the-century sale, etc.

There are two important reasons for this. The first is that it's going to help you draw in people who might have otherwise stayed away. For some people, the deal can't just be good – it has to be so good that they can't pass it up. The state of the economy is less important to them than the percentage discount they'll be receiving.

Another just as important reason is that you want to attach a concrete story to every hefty discount you give. Otherwise, your sale is likely to become permanent. In other words, you want to set those prices apart from your normal offer in some special way because prices tend to be sticky. That is, whatever somebody pays for something one time, they'll expect to pay again next time. If you aren't careful in conveying the message that your offer is a one-time deal or extravaganza, those bargain-hunting customers (and possibly some of your others) are going to keep asking for the discounted price when the economy picks up again – and they're going to refuse to pay a cent more. Obviously, that's a no-win situation for you, so be sure that they understand why you're cutting your prices, and that they know that, whether they take the offer or leave it, they won't be seeing it again in the future.

People often associate recessions with loss, but they can also bring opportunity, and reaching out to bargain hunters is a good example of this. A slow economy offers the perfect excuse to touch base with them and give them a really good reason to buy whatever it was they passed on last time. In fact, if you work things correctly, you might even be able to accomplish a few things at once, taking the chance to clear out some old inventory and establish new relationships at the same time.

Wherever you live and whatever you sell, there's someone out there who's been waiting for the right time to buy. Use the recession as an opportunity to open that door and make some money you wouldn't have gotten otherwise. They'll find a great deal, and you'll find another hidden commission.

CHAPTER NINE
LOOK INTO THE PAST

Now is a good time to close business you didn't get the first time around.

One of the ironies of the selling profession is that we tend to be less efficient when times are good. As ridiculous as it sounds, most of us close far fewer deals – as a percentage – during an economic upswing than we do during a downswing. Why is this? It all comes back to simple supply and demand: when there's lots of money around, we have lots of prospects, so we don't pay as much attention to each one; but when things go south, every sale means a little more, not to mention there are fewer of them to go around, so we put our maximum effort into every potential deal.

The net of all of this is that you probably have a number of contacts that could have been closed in the past, but weren't. In some cases, they might have been prospects that required a great deal of individual attention, or necessitated a specialized product or proposal to meet their needs. Or, it might be that they were smaller customers who found a better deal or more attention elsewhere. In any case, they represent money that got away.

If there's one thing to do in a recession, it's collect all of that loose change and put it to work. Does that mean you're suddenly going to be able to close all of these new prospects? Probably not. But it does mean that now is a good time to call them, especially when you consider that the competition might not. And besides, you've probably got a lot fewer new leads coming in, so why not?

Recognize this is likely to be a low percentage affair. For the most part, customers, or potential customers, that got away did so for good reasons. Many of them will already have bought from someone else. And even amongst those that haven't, the majority are unlikely to be looking to make new purchases in a soft economy. Even so, there are probably going to be a few who are interested in hearing what you have to say, and your previous contact with them means that you're not starting from scratch.

As you get in touch with your existing contacts, be sure to take good notes and see if you can apply any of the strategies you already mentioned. Do they ask about prices and discounts? Then maybe they're bargain hunters who would be interested in hearing about which products you've marked down. Are they worried about the future? Then you might be able to sell them a product or solution that helps them protect their existing purchases or inventory. Have they already made a large investment? Perhaps you can use a "sell small" strategy to earn their day-to-day business.

The point is to exercise your common sense and follow the one rule of selling in any economy: give the customer what they want and need. These tactics work for all kinds of new clients, so why not employ them when dealing with accounts that got away?

Contacting your existing customers and prospects can benefit you in a couple of ways. On the one hand, it can bring you fresh revenue and accounts without eating up a lot of your time. After all, you probably have varying degrees of knowledge about the wants and needs of each person on the list, so you don't have to reinvent the wheel with every conversation. And at the same time, it gets you into the habit of doing better follow up, meaning that you'll sell more efficiently when things pick up.

Your existing contact list can be a gold mine in a recession... or it could be worth very little. A lot depends on how many names you have, and how well you work the strategies we've already covered. But don't miss out on some of the easiest potential sales you can make; go through those familiar faces and see if you can't find someone who was close to buying before, because you might be able to make something happen now.

CHAPTER TEN
LEARN NEW TRICKS

A tough economy will separate those who can learn and adapt from those who are going out of business.

One of the interesting things about a recession is that it quickly separates those individuals and companies who can adapt from those who can't. And in every case, those who can manage and deal with change are going to come out on top. So far, we've been looking at ways that this applies to dealing with your existing and prospective customers. But innovative organizations and producers won't stop there – they'll start looking for new methods of finding and attracting new prospects.

For that reason, it's a good idea to give some thought about where your new customers have been coming from in the past. Most salespeople, and the companies they work for, tend to stick with what they know. Whether it's print ads, television marketing, or an extensive direct mail campaign, they have a system that they feel works, and so they're hesitant to let it go –*even though the environment around them is changing.*

These are easy ways of finding new clientele. They're also pretty expensive. And what's more, these strategies usually bring declining results in a soft economy, because they're reactive. As people notice they have less and less available income to spend, they pay less attention to the advertisements they see in the media. In other words, since consumers aren't in the mood to go shopping, these blanket marketing efforts become little more than background noise.

The easiest way to counteract this problem is to engage in more hands-on, cost-effective marketing campaigns. This isn't to say that you should immediately ditch your advertising budget, but it does mean you should take a hard look at the return you're getting from those expenditures. Are those TV commercials flooding your store business with new customers? Are the newspaper ads filling out the balance sheet? If the answer to either of those questions is a resounding "yes," then don't stop what's working. But if you aren't sure you're getting your money's worth, then consider some other avenues to finding new business.

For many types of companies, the Internet can be a great source of new revenue. You don't have to have a flashy, expensive website to get business online. In fact, with a little bit of effort in the form of pay per click ads, business blogs, website coupons, and partnership arrangements, you can find a new stream of virtual customers for practically nothing.

Another good strategy is to amend your current advertising and marketing campaigns to encompass the themes we've already examined. Offer coupons in your print ads, or use television spots to bring in those bargain hunters. The key is to amend your message so that it speaks to customers who have a recession mindset.

While these are good ideas, I realize that many or most of the men and women reading this book don't control their company's advertising budget and direction. In that case, you're stuck with whatever your sales manager or media director decides to do. But even though you might not be in control of your company's marketing, you can still direct your own in the most efficient and effective way possible.

To do that, you might have to dust off some skills you haven't used for awhile, if you've ever used them at all. That's because the most cost-effective ways of finding new business – the so-called "guerrilla tactics" that work on effort, not money – are rarely practiced by many of today's biggest companies. They're hard work, so they've fallen out of favor to more elegant and more expensive techniques over the past couple of decades.

The first of these is the dreaded cold call. For many salespeople, this very phrase incites fear, panic, and the desire to leap from a tall building. There's good reason for that; cold calling can be a difficult and frustrating activity. But there's a reason that millions of salespeople have relied on it for decades, too: it works. It's a mathematical certainty that if you speak to enough people, you're going to find one who's ready, willing, and able to buy from you. This is true in any economy, regardless of what you sell. If you want stay in business, picking up the phone is a guaranteed way to do it.

For the truly brave, classical door-to-door cold calling is also an option. Again, many people will shun this recommendation, and they are half right. When they tell you that going door-to-door is going to get you more rejections than anything else, that's the truth. And when they say that most people won't buy from someone they don't know, they're on the money again. But what's missing from this picture is the reality that, again, if you talk to enough people, you're still going to sell something. And more than that, you might even make a few great clients. That's because technology has created an environment where most people rarely see the professionals they do business with – something we'll be talking about in just a moment – leaving an opening for the men and women who are willing to shake a few hands.

The key to successful cold calling, in person or over the phone, is consistency. Unless you're very lucky, you're probably not going to make a big sale after just a few phone calls or visits. It does happen, but those situations are rare. What's more likely is that you'll make a handful of new contacts every day, until you eventually end up with a sales pipeline filled with qualified prospects. In other words, it's not going to happen overnight; but it is going to happen, and it's going to cost you very little except for your time. That's what makes cold calling such a valuable tool in a recession.

Asking for referrals is another great no-cost way to find new people. Many salespeople are afraid to hit up their customers for referrals, but if you've done a good job for them, why not? You could even gain a couple of referrals with a small sales strategy. Your clients might not know anybody who's looking to make a big purchase or investment, but they could have a friend or acquaintance who needs a service plan for their existing product, or has some ongoing small need for what you do. Isn't it worth it to make a few calls and find out?

For even more variety in recession prospecting, try holding seminars. Inviting a few dozen people to your office for an informational session on ways they can save money in a tough economy is a great way to get in front of a few new faces. Best of all, you can do it for the price of a few cups of coffee. Likewise, sending out a newsletter with a few informational tips can be a great way to create awareness. You can even save on printing and postage costs by distributing it online.

There are probably dozens or hundreds of other promotional techniques that you can pick up from books or by talking with experienced sales and marketing professionals. But at the end of the day, what you need to do is find a handful of methods that you can use effectively and consistently. If you're going to weather a recession in good shape, I suggest you try the few we've outlined here. They're all easy, and they all work. None of them will cost you more than a few hours and some spare change, but they just might keep a steady stream of new accounts coming your way.

CHAPTER ELEVEN
GO HUNTING

If your business is hurting, then your competition might be hurting worse. Take advantage by picking up some of their customers.

Recessions have a way of throwing companies, especially big ones, into disarray. If your competitors have been cutting staff, missing delivery deadlines, holding back new products, or trimming their customer service, then now could be the perfect time to go after their customers.

This is especially true if you're working in an industry that's been hit really hard by the recession. You might be wondering how you're going to increase or even maintain your sales when there is simply less business to be found. The answer is that you're going to do it by grabbing a bigger piece of the smaller pie – you're going to get your customers, and your competitors', too.

Pay attention, and it might even be easier than you think. That's because your biggest competitors – the behemoths that eat up the lion's share of the business in your industry – are probably hurting. Chances are, they're laying off workers, cutting back on services, and doing whatever else they can to cut costs. Big businesses can't move nimbly. Because of their size and hefty market share, they tend to hire lots of new people during an economic expansion. Once a recession comes, though, they're forced to backtrack and shed excess employees. Those changes mean their customers are more vulnerable than ever. Now could be the perfect time to move in and start picking up accounts.

This can work for a couple of reasons. The first is that an overall change in personnel means that lots of details are going to be lost in the shuffle. For instance, it might be that a certain number of accounts are moving from one representative to another. In that case, the customer doesn't have any relationship with the person who's now handling their business. With no personal ties to their supplier, they're more likely than ever to consider jumping to another firm.

At the same time, lots of corporations shed many of their front-line customer service employees at the first sign of a downturn. What this means to you is that their clients are now waiting longer to have their problems and issues resolved. How happy do you think that makes them with your competitor? That's why it's so important that you get in touch with them during this time.

A third reason businesses lose ground in a recession is that they put off proposed investments and improvements. Where they might have planned a new product rollout, or a new line of services, they choose instead to keep their existing offerings in place, or even start instituting new fees and charges. If you or your company can push forward and launch something innovative, then you're probably well positioned to pick up new business. Keep in mind, too, that this doesn't necessarily mean that you have to come up with a new or unique technology. Lots of times you can get a leg up on your competitor simply by virtue of keeping up your existing fee schedule or improvement package in place; all you have to do is find the areas where other companies aren't keeping up and exploit those weaknesses.

More often than not, you won't have to look that far to find them. In the beginning and middle stage of a recession, job losses, factory closings, and other cutbacks are all over the news. It won't be hard for you – or your customers and prospects – to see what's going on in the world. If you've heard that a really big company is laying off 10% of their staff, then chances are good so have that company's customers. They might not be sure what this means to them and their accounts, but you can help them figure it out.

Remember, though, that there are two sides to this equation. Just as a recession is the ideal time to grab business from your competitors, it's just as easy for you to lose the business you have. This is especially true if you or your employer are the ones letting people go or offering fewer services. Realize that any of these actions is going to create a negative impression in the public – one that's going to filter down to your existing customers and prospects. Make sure you get in touch with each and every one of them to explain what's going on. They might have questions or doubts about your ability to continue to serve them. And while you might not be able to completely reassure them, it's better that they discuss those issues with you than another salesperson who sees an opportunity.

The lesson in all of this is that an economic downturn brings chaos, and the bigger the company, the more frantic and disorganized things are going to be. So, if you work in an industry that seems to be sinking like the Titanic, take heart: there might be fewer sales to be made, but you can more than make up for that by grabbing a bigger piece of the pie. All you have to do is pay attention to which of your competitors is falling apart, and then be there to help their customers pick up the pieces.

CHAPTER TWELVE
BE INFORMED

By paying attention, and looking for clues, you can find out who's still buying.

You've probably noticed that one of the themes throughout this book is that families and businesses don't stop spending in a recession; they're just more careful about what they buy. In other words, they'll still make the right purchase in your investment, but it has to make sense for them.

To that end, it makes sense to have your offers and proposals be as specific as they can be. The more you know about your clients, the better chance you stand of being able to present them with solutions that speak to their needs, especially when they're craving answers for their own recession-impacted businesses.

As an example, suppose you know that one of your biggest prospects, a manufacturer of building supplies, has just opened an overseas plant to save money on production costs. Do you think this information could help you sell them a new line of training materials? What about foreign currency hedges, international legal consulting, or even telecommunications equipment?

I'm sure you could think of dozens of other products and services that might be a good fit, but the point isn't what any specific company is doing, or what in particular you might sell them – it's that knowing what's going on with your customers and prospects gives you an opportunity to offer something that fits them perfectly. To pull it off, though, you're going to need to know more than just a name and phone number. Luckily, there's a wealth of free research out there for sales professionals to find.

First off, there are the thousands of stories that appear in the press. Major investments, initiatives, and restructurings are almost always reported in business journals. A quick scan through their pages will often give you a good taste of what's going on in a community or business region. And by visiting local business publications online, you can even search through articles for names and topics.

Trade magazines represent the same kind of information, but usually for an industry rather than an area. So if most of your clients are scattered around the country, but are in similar or related businesses, then looking through these publications is a great idea. Not only will they give you an idea of who is doing well, but they'll also convey a sense of what the trends in that field are. And as an added bonus, trade magazines frequently run profiles of top executives and companies, detailing personal and company information which you can use to put together a strong proposal.

When it comes to looking for names, or finding out more about a specific prospect, few tools can rival the power of the Internet. Through company websites, news outlets, and even pages posted by vendors and colleagues, you can find out almost anything you'd want to know about the men and women you wish to sell to. It's not uncommon for businesses to have information like their staff directory, annual sales, or monthly meeting calendar posted online for everyone to see. So why not take a few minutes looking around for information that can guide you towards a sale?

And while you're at it, don't just stop at the obvious business websites. Business and social networking sites like Facebook, LinkedIn, and Myspace can be good stops for gathering more data. Much of what you find probably won't be that pertinent, but every once in a while you'll discover a CEO who went to the same college as you, or a VP who shares your passion for fly fishing. None of these tidbits is going to close the deal for you, but every piece of information you have inches you closer.

Learning to find information in magazines, company reports, and on the Internet will probably take you a little longer than you're used to spending on your lists at first. But with a little practice, you'll soon find that you can unlock an enormous amount of insight with just a few turns of a page or clicks of a mouse. As you do, take careful notes. You don't have to be looking for any one fact in particular; the point is to find out as much as you can about your customers. From there, you can take what you've learned and use it to tailor your approach.

In fact, the best advice is probably to learn to dig below the surface – start to see your clients and prospects in the context of their own businesses and industries. For example, you'll recall from the first couple of chapters that anything to do with the economy has a sort of chain effect. With that in mind, you don't just want to know what's going on with your client, but also what's going on with your client's clients, and so on. Knowing that your customer's biggest customer is struggling tells you a lot about the situation. So does finding out that their largest supplier is expanding, or closing up shop. In either case, digging a little deeper allows you to help them solve a problem or situation that might be looming just over the horizon. And once you can do that, you're not another salesperson trying to make money – you're a professional who can help them get through the recession.

Lots of salespeople know only as much about their customers and prospects as they've written on an information card. And in good times, you might be able to make a living this way. But to thrive in a recession, you have to give people the answers to their problems. Take advantage of the wealth of information that's available about the people you want to do business with. Because by keeping yourself informed, you're keeping yourself in business.

CHAPTER THIRTEEN
ADD A PERSONAL TOUCH

In tough times, people are quick to get rid of vendors;

but they hardly ever fire a friend and trusted advisor.

How many of your customers could pick you out of a lineup? If your answer is anything other than "all of them," then you've got some work to do. Take advantage of the break in business that a recession affords by getting in front of your customers. A quick lunch, or even a cup of coffee, is a good way to remind people why they're doing business with you in the first place. It's also a good way to renew relationships and play defense against budget cuts and competing firms.

In the same way you can shrug off the effects of a recession by bringing in more new accounts, you can make things twice as bad by losing the ones you already had. We've mentioned this briefly already, but we skipped over the single biggest tool in your customer-retention arsenal: *personal attention.*

People love to be the center of attention, especially when they're making purchases. Most salespeople realize this, and become masters at showering their prospects and new customers with their undivided focus. Once the sale is completed, though, it's not unusual for the customer to fade into the background. Weekly calls and prompt proposals are replaced by monthly reports and quarterly check-ins.

To a certain degree, this is normal and unavoidable. After all, as a professional salesperson, you're paid to open new accounts. If you spent all your time chatting it up with existing customers, you wouldn't be able to make your quotas – or any money, for that matter. Still, for many customers the completion of the sale feels like the end of a honeymoon. They start to miss the concern and attention to detail you showed them when you were still courting them as a customer. So it's no surprise that, when another salesperson seems to be working overtime to earn their account, they're tempted to stray.

Use the lull in business to reignite the fire. Make a list of all your customers, from your biggest on down to your smallest, and make appointments to see each and every one of them face-to-face. If possible, try to meet them for a one-on-one lunch. If your schedule or budget doesn't allow for that, however, see if you can meet them for coffee, or even just a few minutes in their office.

When you arrive, be prepared. Don't show up expecting to discuss the weather or your local sports team. A little bit of small talk is okay, but you should use your time to bring forth a few ideas on ways your customer can save money or be more profitable in a recession. Remember, you're not the only one hurting from a tough economy; your clients and colleagues are feeling the pinch, too. Try to help them find ways to ride out the storm.

This is one good use for all of those research skills you should be practicing. Your customers might be overwhelmed with internal problems or even personal issues that arise with a recession. By devoting a bit of time to studying their situation, along with the challenges they face, you might be able to lend a new perspective to the issues with which they're grappling. And the fact that you've done it without their asking speaks volumes about your commitment to working with them. So try to find new answers to your customers' existing – or forthcoming – problems. At the very least, it will give you something to talk about.

At the same time, be careful in pitching too many of your own products and solutions. If your clients haven't seen your face for a very long time, don't give them the impression that you're just stopping by to sell something. Make it clear that you care about them and their business, and that you're just touching base to see how they're doing.

This might seem like you're passing up a good sales opportunity, and that's possible. But getting some personal time with your customers is about playing defense. Recessions are times of transition; it's easier for your clients to decide to work with someone else when it seems like drastic changes are needed just to keep up. But they're a lot less likely to fire someone they know and trust, so be sure you fit that bill.

Having good relationships with your clients pays you back twice: first, when the recession comes and they don't drop you as a vendor or supplier; and secondly when the economy turns around again and they remember the personal attention you showed them when times were tight. You can be sure your customers will remember how you try to help them stick it out rather than make a quick buck.

Don't let the people you work for wonder if you've gone missing. Spend a recession giving them the best service they've ever had. It might not be the fastest way to bring in new customers, but it will stop you from losing the ones you have.

CHAPTER FOURTEEN
GET BACK TO BASICS

Stay focused on the reasons people should buy from you,

and they will.

What is it that your company does better than any other? What service do you provide, or what qualifications do you bring, that make you stand out from everyone else in the marketplace? Lots of salespeople can't say, but knowing and understanding the answers to these questions is the key to thriving when things are slow, because they'll tell you who's likely to buy from you in *any* economy.

I understand if you think this sounds overly simplistic. After all, who doesn't know what they do? Even so, I'd advise you to take a moment to think about where your competitive advantages actually lie. That's because lots of companies, in the middle of an economic boom, decide to branch out a little. That is, tempted by the possibility of record profits, they test new products and markets to see which ones they can play in, and which they can't.

Frequently, this is driven by the desire of executives or shareholders to grab a piece of whatever fad or trend is hot at the moment. It's the reason you'll sometimes see odd combinations of concepts, like pet food stores with an internet focus, or ice cream flavors named after animated movie characters; somebody at the top of those companies saw a chance to make some money in a growing segment of the economy.

Some of these expansions and cross-promotions work out; others don't. But regardless of their immediate success and failure, these ventures are a bit dangerous because they distract the public – not to mention the sales staff – from the company's real mission. And when times get tough, you can be sure that customers won't care if you sell swimming pool products with your copiers, or tires along with PCs. They might have indulged those impulse purchases when the dollars were flowing, but what they'll come to you for now is the one thing you're known for, because that's where your actual value is. In a recession, people don't want fluff; they want strong service and integrity, a quality product, or a guarantee that your service is going to be delivered as promised.

So think about what your company's reputation is. If what comes to mind would take you longer than a few seconds to say out loud, then throw that away and start again, because it's too complicated. When you hit on your strength, it should jump out at you right away, because it won't just tell you *what* people are buying from you — it will also tell you *why*.

The core value or unique selling proposition is going to be different for every business out there. In some cases, firms are competing on value. In other words, they might not be the cheapest, but their product lasts the longest, or does the most. Other companies fly high because they're strong on service; when you buy from them, you don't have to worry that you're going to be stuck with a problem you can't solve, because they'll take care of everything for you. Still other businesses thrive on their location, convenience, hours of operation, or even price. It's not uncommon to hear business types claim to look down on those who always work to be the lowest-cost, but there's nothing wrong with that. It's a defined market and one that can do well – especially in a recession.

Be aware that most companies only compete in one or sometimes two of these areas. Nobody expects the supplier that delivers the best product to be the cheapest, or vice versa. Your prospects and customers already know who you are, so give that to them and don't try to be something else. Your company's reputation can give you a strong advantage in a recession by allowing you to offer something known, but only if you're selling your company in a way that's consistent with what people already think of you.

If you're still not sure what your basic pitch is, then check out your company's mission statement. Is this a bit obvious? Sure, but it might remind you of how the organization was built up and what values were emphasized. Chances are, those are the same impressions most customers have of your company. Another way to narrow things down is by asking your customers. Simply find one or two of them you enjoy working with and ask them the magic question, "why do you buy from us?" The insight they'll give you is worth its weight in gold, and it can go a long way towards steering you to new business.

Don't stop with your company, either. When you're looking to find your core strengths, consider yourself. You might have dozens, hundreds, or even thousands of other salespeople working at your firm, so how did you come to your client base? For some people, this will be as simple as a geographic territory, or the fact that they were assigned certain accounts. For most of us, though, there is a certain kind of client that we seek out and do well with over and again.

A recession is a great time to find out who those people are, as well as their needs and challenges. By understanding how and why you're able to work with the people you do, you can go a long way towards finding more like them. Maybe there's some unique aspect of your background, experience, education, or personality that's helping you to reach people. Once you find your individual advantages, play to them. Make sure every prospecting call, appointment, negotiation and close reflect the things you and your company do best.

In a recession, people look for things that are safe, not risky. For that reason, your company's reputation and your own can be enormous assets if you use them correctly. Give people what they want and expect from you, whether it be price, value, service, or something else altogether, and you might just find that the competition isn't as fierce as you thought.

CHAPTER FIFTEEN
GIVE A LITTLE MORE

By adding value, rather than cutting prices, you can keep your income rising through a recession.

The title of this chapter, "Give a Little More," is meant to serve as a reminder of one of the best ways to keep business rolling in during a recession. But it could have just as easily been called "Cut a Little Less," because that's the real problem at play.

Most salespeople understand that people buy solutions, not products, and that prices are only one part of those solutions. And yet, at the first sign of a belt-tightening, they go straight to price cuts in order to close more business – even when price might not be the most pertinent issue. There are lots of ways to keep winning business in a recession, and cutting your margins should be an option of last resort.

In an earlier chapter, we looked at bargain hunters – those folks who refuse to buy from you unless they are getting the absolute, rock bottom, best deal possible. When the economy is in the tank, it makes sense to reach out to these people and speak their language. Holding special sales is a great way to clear out inventory and pull in some sales that you wouldn't have gotten otherwise.

But you have to be careful, because one sale is likely to beget another. If you advertise your prices as "crazy," then it's only a matter of time before your biggest competitors have gone "insane." And sooner or later, you'll both be downright loony – slashing prices so severely that there's little or no profit margin left in the equation. So, if you decide you're going to compete on price, keep this in mind: once you get caught in a tug of war with a competitor over who can give the best deal, there's nowhere to go but down.

Once you get caught in this kind of conundrum, you have a serious problem. That's because your normal customers – the ones who were looking for value, even if it wasn't necessarily at the lowest price – have either moved on or become bargain hunters themselves. This is why it's so important that you appeal to bargain hunters in the right way; you can make some extra sales with them, but you risk the most profitable part of your business.

Besides, there are a lot of ways to keep drawing in budget-conscious buyers without resorting to fire sales and other emergency tactics. One of the simplest is to start offering more for the money. Just take whatever you are offering before, and add more to it at the same price. What you decide to give isn't the point, but in-house products usually offer the best cost-to-value ratio.

Value is a subjective thing. The actual cost of an extra item isn't important; its worth to the customer is. That's why extended warranties, add-on products, and service guarantees work so well. They aren't likely to cost you or your company very much money, but offering them is of definite benefit for your customers. And more often than not, throwing in bonus products or upgrades won't cut nearly as far into your commissions – or your sales manager's patience – as an outright price cut would.

You can also add value the old-fashioned way: with your time. Your customers work with a sales professional, rather than buying wholesale or over the Internet, because they need help and guidance. You work with your products or services every day, so you know more about them and their uses than the people who buy from you. By arranging a schedule of follow-up appointments, offering a few hours of consulting, or otherwise sharing your knowledge, you can instantly create value without losing a single cent.

Of course, there are going to be times when these methods won't work. Either because your customers just don't have the money, or because they've gotten lower quotes from other suppliers, you might have to discount whatever you're selling. And really, that's just the way a recession works. All you can do is work the numbers, talk to your sales manager if necessary, and decide the best way to go forward. If it's the only way to make a sale or keep a customer, then there are times you do what you have to do – and anyone who tells you otherwise probably hasn't sold in a soft economy. But try to hold firm to your prices by giving a little more, and leave discounts as your last resort. It won't be easy, but you will probably find that you can close most deals this way without giving away the farm.

As a final thought along those lines, remember to think of the long-term when you're contemplating a deep price cut. There does come a point in negotiating the sale where you can win the battle, but lose the war. In other words, even in a tough economy, there are some orders you're better off walking away from. Giving huge discounts now teaches clients to ask for them in the future, so think long and hard about whether it's worth it to make a deal now if it's going to haunt you later.

There is one group that is exempted from this rule, however: those companies we talked about in the last chapter who compete mainly on price. If you know that your customers buy from you because you're charging the least, then a recession is an especially great time to remind them of those savings. In fact, one of your biggest challenges won't be keeping prices up, it will be making sure you aren't being undercut by competitors. So by all means, cut, slash, and burn your prices to the ground. You might find that customers who weren't as receptive to you before are all ears now. Families, managers, and business owners alike are under pressure to get what they need for less money. This is your day – make hay while the sun shines.

CHAPTER SIXTEEN
IMPROVE YOUR SKILLS

You should come out of a recession as a better salesperson than you went in.

In some ways, a recession is a little like a high school study hall for salespeople – things are pretty quiet, and you probably aren't expected to be doing all that much. This makes it the perfect time to increase your sales skills. With the pressure off, you're free to try out new methods and techniques. If they work, you can integrate them into your routine and use them to pick up some new business. If they don't, you haven't lost anything for the effort.

Make no mistake, we all have areas where we could stand to improve. I have yet to meet a salesperson who couldn't benefit from knowing or understanding a little bit more about their customers or their line of work. The good news, though, is that a lot of really talented and thoughtful men and women have come before you. And to help guide you on your way, they've left hundreds of books, audio seminars, and even video presentations. Any one of them can help you make more money. Your sales manager might even have some of their favorites sitting around the office; all you have to do is invest a little bit of your time.

Lots of sales people miss out on these opportunities because they think can't spare the extra minutes. If you fall in that category, think about it this way: suppose you devoted just an hour a day to improving your sales career. Over the course of the year, that would amount to dozens of books to read, more than fifty audio courses listened to, or two hundred DVDs watched. Do you honestly think that kind of effort wouldn't make an enormous difference in your selling ability?

Like cold calling or other cumulative techniques, the key to making a sales education effort work is doing a little bit every day. You can't decide to sit down and read three dozen books in a row – you'd get burnt out quickly and wouldn't learn anything. But by moving forward in tiny increments, you let your mind absorb small bits of knowledge that you can use in everyday selling situations.

And you don't have to stop with materials that are strictly "sales related." A top salesperson has to be fluent in many areas, including prospecting, product knowledge, negotiation, public speaking, and written communication. If you really want to be on the top of your game, you could also add other areas like fashion or psychology, since dressing for success and understanding other people's motivations can help you make those extra sales that separate the superstars from the average performers.

You could probably think of another handful of topics that can be helpful in your own sales career off the top of your head, and I would encourage you to pursue those, as well. The point, however, is that sales is a craft – you should always be improving as a professional. The moment you stop growing and learning, you resign yourself to never making any more money than you are right now.

Like several of the other techniques in this book, you'll only get half the benefit right away. Sure, spending the time to read books like this one will probably help you make more sales in the short term. The real payoff, though, comes down the road. For one thing, it will probably take you several months or longer to integrate the new lessons you're learning into your everyday work habits. At the same time, you'll become a much stronger, more efficient salesperson by the time the economy turns around. And finally, showing a little bit of extra effort can't help but make you look better to your supervisors. Managers know who on their staff is reaching for the next level and which producers are drifting through each day. Show a bit of ambition in your career, and you'll guarantee yourself a place, not to mention a future, with your current employer.

A lot of what you're going to get out of your job during a recession, and after, depends on what you're willing to put in. If you see it as a chance to goof off, then you'll probably see your sales go in the tank. But if you treat it like an opportunity to get better at your job, you come out the other side ready to move to the head of the class.

CHAPTER SEVENTEEN
GET ORGANIZED

In a tough economy, you can't afford to lose sales because

you can't manage your time.

Even the slightest hint of a recession will send businesses and families looking for a place to cut expenses. Most salespeople, though, will fail to take stock of their most precious resource – time. Make sure you don't make the same mistake. By learning to work more efficiently, you can make up the productivity gap you feel when times are tough.

How many hours a week should you spend at work, whether it's in the office or on the road? The majority of commissioned sales professional out there are putting in more than forty or fifty hours, especially when they're trying to overcome the challenge of a tighter economy. And yet, when you take away the amount of time they spend on unimportant activities, most of them spend less than half their week doing things that actually matter. This isn't to imply that they're lazy, or that they aren't working hard enough. In fact, it's incredibly common for salespeople to be working their brains out, and still get very little done.

That's because most people in any profession are poor managers of their own time. Companies realize this, and spend millions each year trying to recoup the revenue that's lost with poor clock management. But while poor organization might effect everyone from accountants to maintenance staff, it's especially destructive to salespeople, since they're paid for the amount of business they generate. Losing time means losing calls and meetings, which translates into smaller paychecks. So have no doubt, being disorganized can cost you a big chunk of change.

Again, this is a problem that is often masked by a robust economy. When new accounts and business are flying around everywhere, there's not much time to think about whether you're working efficiently. It's an ironic fact: time-wasting habits actually cost you more when you're busy, but you're making too much money to think about it. In other words, you're doing well, just not as well as you could be.

In a recession, though, inefficiency isn't just wasteful – it can put you out of business. Earlier in the book, we looked at generating more activity as a way to overcome the recession. If you have sloppy work habits, that's going to be even harder to do, because you probably don't even know where your days are going.

Learning to master your working hours is one of those things that can make or break your sales career. This isn't a book about time management, but I can offer some basic advice for getting more out of your day.

First of all, be clear about what you're actually trying to do. How many sales do you want to make this year? Once you have that number in mind, write it down on a piece of paper and start to work backwards. How many monthly sales are called for in order to meet your yearly goal? How does that average out per week, or even every day?

When you've figured those numbers out – either from experience, or just an educated guess – continue to work backwards in an even more specific framework. Calculate what you'll need to do every day to get there. You probably have a good idea of how many proposals you have to give to close a new order, how many cold calls it takes to find a qualified customer to make a proposal to, and so on. From there, it's all simple math. It might be that you need to make five calls, ask three people for a referral, or do something else altogether. How you're drumming up business doesn't matter; your awareness of how much of it you have to do in order to stay on the job does.

Once you figured that out, the hard part is going to be keeping yourself focused and not becoming distracted by what's going on all around you. The first way to accomplish that is to simply set aside some time by coming into the office a bit earlier or leaving a little later. If you know that you need to make half a dozen cold calls each morning to pay your mortgage, then by all means do it first, before things pick up and you get too busy.

The second way to find more time is to waste less of it. We all wish we had more hours in the day, but the truth is that we usually squander half the ones we do have by burning them on the phone, surfing the Internet during business hours, shuffling through a disorganized work space, sitting in long meetings, and dealing with other interruptions that could be handled more quickly. The best way to improve your time management skills is by taking a seminar or reading a good book on the topic and then applying what you've learned. Most salespeople are missing a lot of productive hours, and thos losses are coming straight out of their commission checks.

Treat a recession the same way you would a diet – as a chance to trim some of the fat out of your day. It won't be easy, but you might just find that you breathe easier without all those bad habits in the way.

CHAPTER EIGHTEEN
ADD TO YOUR TEAM

There are people out there who can help you get through

a recession, and many of them are looking for work.

If you've been meaning to bring someone new into your team, and can afford the cash outlay, a recession might be the perfect time to do it. Why? For starters, bigger firms tend to "throw out the baby with the bath water," meaning you might finally get that superstar your office has needed. Better yet, because the economy has cooled off, you might get them for a lot less than you otherwise would, and have the opportunity to train them without the pressures of a busy, overworked environment.

If you're any good at what you do, then your time is valuable. I don't mean that in a "carpe diem" way - although that's certainly good advice in any language - but in a bottom-line sense. You've been trained to close new sales that bring hundreds or thousands of dollars into your company. Every second that you're not doing that, each moment that you're not in front of a qualified prospect, you're bringing in less money than you could be.

It's astonishing how few salespeople know what they're actually worth. Let's suppose that you see three people a day, bringing in one new account worth ten thousand dollars in new revenue. What's more profitable for you and your company: for you to be meeting qualified prospects, or to have you on the phone dealing with a mundane customer service issue?

You've probably realized this before, even if it was just implicitly. Why waste your time doing routine chores when you could be earning commissions? The fact is, most salespeople burn their time on inefficient tasks because they don't have a choice; they just don't have the help they need.

Well, now might be the time to get it. As your colleagues and competitors rush to downsize their staffs, a lot of qualified people are going to be available. Best of all, you won't have to pay huge hiring bonuses to get them. It's not unusual to find sales assistants, cold callers, receptionists, typists, and every other form of support staff changing jobs in the early stages of a recession. Finding them is as easy as asking a few friends, or placing an ad in a magazine or online.

A word of caution, though: don't forget to check out your potential new hires before you sign on the dotted line. Look over resumes and call references. Your competitors aren't stupid (well, they might be, but we'll give them the benefit of the doubt) – they probably aren't going to lay off their star employees first. As with any cutback, it's the most unproductive folks who are going to at the outset.

Fortunately for you, your competitors don't always know who that unproductive candidate actually is. Especially in larger companies and departments, managers are forced to make snap decisions about who to let go – or even have those decisions made for them by someone in accounting or human resources. One of their best workers could be released because of a lack of seniority, or for not being a regular at the boss's poker game. Take advantage by using the recession to pick up the help you need.

Bringing in talented people without paying a fortune is a good enough reason to go looking, but if you wanted another one, consider this: a recession is the perfect time to train someone new. Most companies will hire in a boom, because the economics are such that they'll see a quick return. If you're pretty confident about your industry, though, you can do better by grabbing someone when things are slow. Instead of throwing them to the fire at a time when you're both likely to be swamped, you can use the lull in the action to ease them into the position and get them familiar with your working habits.

Using this time to train someone personally can really cut the learning curve required to integrate them. More importantly, it can allow them to be ready to pitch in when business is back in full swing. Things are going to turn around sooner or later, and you'll want your new assistant or cold caller helping you sell – not figuring out where the copier is.

All kinds of companies, big and small, are going to look to cut costs and labor when a recession hits. In their rush to scale back, they're going to make some mistakes. If you can keep a cool head and a long-term perspective, then you might just be able to snag an outstanding employee who is looking for a new opportunity.

CHAPTER NINETEEN
BUY LOW

Recessions mean bargains, so it might be a great time to make an investment at rock-bottom prices.

Just as a few of your customers will be bargain-hunting during a recession, so should you be. While most firms and salespeople will understandably look to make fewer purchases during a recession, the smartest handful realize that there are still deals to be had. In fact, you might not ever find a better time to upgrade the equipment, software, or services you need to grow your business.

Remember, the first impulse of any salesperson or business owner facing down an economic hiccup will be to cut their prices. They know it's a sure way to bring in customers, and while I advise you to be careful about following their lead, that doesn't mean you shouldn't profit from the tendency. That's because practically anything you need or could use is going to be on sale. So, if you have the money to buy – and if you're following the advice in this book, you should – now is a good time to dive in.

That's not to say you should act like you just won the lottery. We all know someone who will buy a ridiculous product that they don't need, just because "it was on sale." No deal is too good to pass up if you don't have a use for what's being offered. Consider any purchase or investment through the lens of the return or efficiency it will provide. Will a new gadget really save you time, or does it just look more high-tech than the one you have? Can you get by just as well with your existing setup, or would the purchase mean a real upgrade?

These are questions you'll have to answer yourself, but be careful to separate your needs from your wants. In the excitement of finding a great deal, it's easy to get carried away. Buyer's remorse is never as likely to be so strong as it is when the economy is tight, and many items bought on sale or clearance can't be refunded or returned.

While there are no guidelines on what types of products you should buy in a recession, anything involving technology is a good start. Lots of companies will put off releasing new versions of PCs, software, and other productivity tools, while cutting prices on existing stock at the same time. That means there are probably deals to be had on anything on anything that flashes or beeps. You're also likely to find great bargains on clothing, financial products, and office supplies, since normal consumer spending in these areas is probably going to be depressed.

Likewise, the contractors you work with might be eager to offer specials. During a recession, small businesses and the self-employed will often do what they can to hold on to their regular clients. These men and women, like you, are some of the most vulnerable in a soft economy, and they might be willing to trade lower prices for a steady paycheck. If you've got an ongoing need for a service, ask about a prepaid or fixed-fee contract. You may be able to get the outside help you need at a lower price, and help out a vendor at the same time.

When it comes to looking for bargains in a recession, there's not much more to say than "be on the lookout." Good deals are going to be out there, so keep your eyes open for chances to save on the essentials.

CHAPTER TWENTY
PLANT SEEDS

A recession won't last forever, so you need to be ready when things turn around.

Throughout these chapters, I've been giving you a number of tips and techniques designed to help you survive, and even flourish, in a tough economy. But the fact of the matter still remains that there's less going on out there than before. So even though you can do very well in a recession, growing your sales and income, it's critical that you don't lose sight of the forest for the trees.

In a matter of weeks, months, or years, things are going to turn around. You might not even notice the change at first – instead of cutting back, firms will add new employees and initiatives; your orders will get just a bit larger; your customers a fraction more confident. Slowly but surely, the economy is going to right itself. And when that happens, the rest of the world is going to try to catch back up with the sales professionals like yourself who have been working so hard to get ahead.

If you follow the tips in this book, you should be well-positioned to withstand the challenge. Still, a booming economy is going to bring fresh competition, different products, and newly-minted strategies from other salespeople out to grab some of your accounts. With that in mind, spend some of your time in a recession building for the future.

Some of the steps you can take we've already covered. Strengthening your personal relationships is a good start, as is honing your sales skills. You can also make yourself more of an authority in your field by getting more formal education or credentials, networking with industry leaders, or writing opinion pieces for trade magazines and business journals.

You'd also do well to look for business that you can win in the future, even if it's closed off to you now. If one of your biggest prospects tells you that they aren't in a position to act while the economy is soft, take their word for it. But that doesn't mean you should give up on them completely. Practice your research skills to keep tabs on what they're up to as the economy progresses. Forward anything you come across that might be of help to them. These efforts might not pay immediate dividends, but that doesn't mean they're a waste of time. By using their time and energy productively, sales professionals don't just do well in soft markets; they also create opportunities for the future.

Don't just look outside your own walls, either. Cultivate strong relationships within your own company. Learn how other departments work, as well as who wields the authority within them. On the surface, this can help you increase your knowledge about company history, policy and product details. At a deeper level, it can familiarize you with the men and women who are going to be in charge when your company is growing and hiring again. They might even be able to help you secure a promotion leading the new hires that will probably come along with an uptick in the economic picture.

In my opening comments, I advised you to remember that economic cycles are inevitable. If you accept that fact, then upswings are never too far away. Don't get so steeped in recession selling that you miss the boat when things are busy again. Pay attention not only to what your customers are buying now, but what they'll want to buy when they have bigger budgets down the road. Know what products you'll be releasing in the future, and how they stack up against the competition.

Recessions, like any part of the economic cycle, are temporary. Just as grass will eventually grow in the same spot where snow can lie for months, jobs and income don't tend to stay down for long. By keeping your nose to the grindstone, you can power your way through any economic storm; just don't forget to look up and catch the sun when it comes.

CHAPTER TWENTY-ONE
BEAT THE ECONOMY

With the right skills and mindset, a recession can be as profitable as any other time… or even more.

By taking the tips in this book and putting them all together, anybody can turn the tables on a recession and come out better than ever. The most important ingredient, however, is *attitude*. Recessions are real, but they're created largely by our own fears and ideas. With the right mindset, and some simple guidelines, they can be as profitable – or more so – than any other economic climate.

The challenge to you is to adopt that mindset and make it your own. When you're reading these words in a book, that might seem easy to do. But once you put these pages down, a slow economy is still going to be right there waiting for you. What's worse, it's going to bring reinforcements. Most of the news reports and conversations you hear are going to focus on the negative. No news travels like bad news, and fear creates its own momentum.

Do what you need to in order to tune out the gloom and doom. If a television anchor spends too much time talking about a closed plant or factory, turn the channel. If a friend complains about how his or her business is doing, listen politely and then change the subject. If your colleagues say they can't make any sales, encourage them to keep trying. I'm not telling you to ignore the reality; rather, choose the one in which you're going to live. Yes, things are going to be difficult; dwelling on that isn't going to make them any easier.

Every economic period – even a boom – has its winners and losers. Never lose sight of that. What's going on outside your door isn't nearly as important as what's going on between your ears. Jobs, markets, and money will always be in flux; that's their natural state. You can either use that as an excuse to fall behind and get buried, or you can make it into an opportunity to go roaring past your competitors. One of the greatest things about the selling profession is that it allows any man or woman who's willing to do some hard work to have control over his or her own destiny.

Overcoming a recession – beating the economy – isn't that hard to do. It just requires that you keep your chin up, stay calm, and play with the hand you're dealt. To that end, take the tips and tools defined in these chapters and decide which ones work best for you. Maybe you can win by selling small, or it could be that you have a number of bargain hunters in your address book. Perhaps you are the master of the personal touch, or maybe you are going to triumph by developing new, cost-effective ways to attract customers.

The real key to making any of these strategies work is understanding the situation for what it is, and then applying a consistent effort. Personal incomes and global interest rates aren't under your control, but your own efforts and activities are. The only one who can decide whether to make it or not is you.

As general as that advice is, it's the best and most important tip in this book. That's because there's nothing, not a single thing, more important to your career than your enthusiasm for it. Even if your whole industry collapses, your employer goes under and you lose your job, you still have the one thing thousands of companies need: *the desire and ability to sell.*

All human endeavors are part passion and part persistence. A sagging economy might mean less work, but it doesn't have to mean less work for you. Leave the effects of a recession to those salespeople who aren't committed to staying in the game. Before long, they'll be off to other jobs and industries, but you'll still be right where you belong – helping people and making money.

BONUS CHAPTER
A NOTE TO OWNERS AND SALES MANAGERS

Tough times call for strong leadership, and your sales team is going to take their cues from you.

While the bulk of this book is directed towards individual salespeople, I'd like to take a few moments and speak directly to those of you in charge. Any one of your salespeople can take the information outlined in the previous chapters and enjoy great success during a recession, and for their sake, I hope they do. But you're in the unique position of being able to put all of these tips together and form a cohesive strategy for your organization. And besides, most of your employees are going to follow your lead.

So, while each person should be responsible for their own actions and attitudes, you have an added responsibility to lead by example. The producers on your staff, especially the younger ones, are going to take their cues from you. If you act like a soft economy is one of the four horsemen of the apocalypse, so will they. On the other hand, if you exude excitement, or at least a lack of fear, that will go a long way towards showing them that a recession is an event to be dealt with, not a phenomenon to be feared.

Keep that in mind and be aware of the signals you're sending. Don't let your body language or tone of voice belie a lack of confidence. If you still doubt that you and your company can come out ahead in a recession, read this book again. In fact, read it four or five times, if that's what it takes. Do whatever you need to do in order to get comfortable with what's going on and make a plan for the future. There's no room in a tight market for doubters, especially not at the top.

At the same time, don't sugarcoat things for your staff. They can read newspapers, too, so don't try to hide or gloss over what's going on with your company. If job losses or other cutbacks are a possibility, let them hear it from you first. The same goes for your customers. Bad news is always bad news, but it's one thing to find out from a vendor that they're closing offices, scaling back on customer service, or charging new fees; it's another thing altogether to get that information from a news service – or even worse, a competitor. Keep everyone informed and you won't just have a smoother ride, you'll build trust at the same time.

Try to keep things loose. A tense staff is almost never as productive and creative as they could be, and it's not easy to make sales when you feel uptight. Shake things up with contests, promotions or just a fun lunch in the office. A joke here and there isn't going to destroy anyone's focus, and it can help foster a spirit of teamwork amongst your sales staff. Fear can cause people to work together, or it can leave them isolated. Get your group thinking on the same page and they might just come up with some new ideas for dealing with a changing business climate.

Also, maintain an open line of communication with senior management. It's not unusual for executives to lose sight of what's happening "on the ground." For this reason, they can make changes during a recession that aggravate, rather than alleviate the challenges facing your sales team. If you're getting sales quotas that don't make sense, promotions that aren't working, or policies that work against your producers, let somebody know.

Don't be afraid to go to bat for your team when it comes to securing funds for new projects and ideas, either. In some cases, the money might not be available, but you'll never know if you don't ask. Sales is the only part of the company that can bring in new revenue right away, and some of the advice in this book goes beyond the authority of an everyday producer. You might be the only one who can approve a new hire, or give the go-ahead on an investment that could save time or bring new revenue in the future. Obviously, you should be careful with your money – whether it's coming from you or your employer – but don't be afraid to take risks, either.

And finally, remember that getting through a recession isn't just for salespeople. When your team wins, so do you. A manager who can skillfully guide his or her team during an economic downturn – and possibly even increase their department's revenues – is never going to be looking for work. In the same way, an owner who works with his sales team to gain market share during a downturn is going to be nicely poised when the economy picks back up again. Treat your sales staff like they're on your side, because they are.

Great leaders are rarely made in good times, so take good care of the men and women working under you in a recession. Share your hope and confidence with them, and provide guidance where you can. If you can help them take that first step – getting over their doubts and fears – they'll carry you the rest of the way to bigger profits and a better career.

About the Author

Matthew Aaron is a salesperson, economist, and writer from Denver, Colorado. Over the last ten years he's sold financial products, lighted signs, furniture, and professional speaking services, not to mention dozens of other things. Along the way, he's also found the time to write several dozen books and pursue a graduate education in economics.

You can find out more about him and his work at www.matthewaaron.com

Printed in the United States
221403BV00001B/20/P